OUR FOOTPRINT ON EARTH

LET'S EXPLORE SCIENCE

AUTHOR
JEANNE STURM

Rourke
Educational Media
rourkeeducationalmedia.com

www.rourkeeducationalmedia.com

PHOTO CREDITS: © omergenc: footprints; © Tom Nulems: border; © Elena Andreeva: Chapter Heading; © Bart Sadowski: Title Page; © Dimitrije Tanaskovic: Title Page; © Diane Labombarbe: Table of Contents; © Eileen Hart: 4; © photoGartner: 5; © Adam Kazmierski: 6, 7; APCortezJr: 8; © mikeuk: 9; © Thaddeus Robertson: 9; © EGDigital: 10; © Ian Bracegirdle: 11; © Nael Nabil: 12; © David Gunn: 13, 32; © Associated Press: 14, 21; © José Luis Gutiérrez: 15; © Elena Elisseeva: 15; © Mark Pruitt: 15; © Hazlan Abdul Hakim: 16; © Khuong Hoang: 16, 18; © ranplett: 18, 31, 34; © Mayumi Terao: 19; © luoman: 19; © Alexander Hafemann: 23; © Simon Smith: 22; © Jerry Willis: 24; © ooyoo: 24; © kativ: 25; © Dieter Spears: 25; © Bubaone: 26; © Jeremy Mayes: 26; © MaximeVIGE: 27; © Reniw Imagery: 27; © CC2.5 Dani 7C3: 27; © Juan Monino: 28; © JackJelly: 29; © Gautier Willaume: 29; © Michael Krinke: 30; © LyaC: 31; © Michelle Preast: 33; © Natallia Bokach: 34;
© Roman Milert: 35; © Kais Tolmats: 35; © Vasiliki Varvaki: 36; © Nicholas: 37; © Oksana Struk: 37; © Tatiana Popova: 37; © BlackJack3D: 38; © Natthawat Wongrat: 39; © Eric Delmar: 40; © Vassiliy Mikhailin: 41; © Christoph Weihs: 41; © Amanda Rohde: 42; © Heather Nemec: 43; © Gene Chutka: 44; © Mark Stay: 44; © Craig Lopetz: 45

Edited by Kelli L. Hicks

Cover and Interior design by Teri Intzegian

Library of Congress Cataloging-in-Publication Data

Sturm, Jeanne.
  Our footprint on Earth / Jeanne Sturm.
    p. cm. -- (Let's explore science)

  ISBN 978-1-60694-408-0 (hard cover)
  ISBN 978-1-60694-526-1 (soft cover)
  1. Technology--Environmental aspects. 2. Pollution--Juvenile literature. 3. Nature--Effect of human beings on--Juvenile literature. 4. Environmental responsibility--Juvenile literature. I. Title.

  TD194 T67S78 2009
  363.7--dc22

                         2009006078

Rourke Educational Media
Printed in the United States of America,
North Mankato, Minnesota

rourkeeducationalmedia.com

customerservice@rourkeeducationalmedia.com • PO Box 643328 Vero Beach, Florida 32964

Table of Contents

CHAPTER ONE

Your Human Footprint

Think about your average day: the foods you eat, the water you use, and the products you buy. How do you get from place to place? Do you walk or ride your bike when possible, instead of asking for a ride in the car?

Ahhh, a well-deserved ice cream tastes delicious! But do we ever stop to think about the energy that went into making those yummy treats and shipping them to our local stores?

The decisions you make, large and small, determine the effect of your life on the planet—your **human footprint**.

Riding your bike is not only fun, but is also good for the environment.

Your impact on the Earth varies depending on where you live. Some countries make more demands on the environment. The United States, for example, is home to 5 percent of the world's population, but it uses 25 percent of the world's resources.

*The United States has an **ecological footprint** larger than any other nation. Much of this footprint is attributed to life in the big city. Cities have higher levels of air pollution from cars and factories than rural areas. The state of California has the unfortunate distinction of being home to many of the most polluted cities. Los Angeles, California is the most polluted city in America.*

CHAPTER TWO

Fossil Fuels Affect the Environment

Before the **industrial revolution**, our impact on the planet was fairly small. But in the mid-1700s, people began replacing human workers with machines.

Where people had once relied on wind, water, and wood for their energy needs, they now powered their machines with the **fossil fuels** coal, oil, and natural gas.

Power plants that burn coal produce more harmful carbon dioxide than all cars, trucks, planes, and other forms of transportation combined.

Oil rigs, such as this one in the Gulf of Mexico, drill natural gas and oil from far beneath the sea floor.

These fossil fuels were formed hundreds of millions of years ago, and they still contain the carbon that was present in the organisms when they died. This carbon is what makes them a source of energy.

But when we burn coal, oil, and natural gas for fuel, too much carbon enters the atmosphere at one time. The carbon combines with oxygen to form carbon dioxide (CO_2), a **greenhouse gas**.

Greenhouse gases are contributing to **global warming** because they trap more of the Sun's energy in the Earth's atmosphere.

Have you ever been late to something because you were stuck in traffic? For you, heavy traffic is a temporary problem. But for the Earth, all the carbon dioxide (CO_2) created by traffic jams is a long-term problem.

Smoke

Steam

Cooling towers, like the ones shown here at the Cottam Power Station, release steam into the atmosphere. Many people mistake the steam, or waste heat, for greenhouse gases. The white smoke shown at the top of the photo is coming from the smoke stack. This smoke is a greenhouse gas.

Our dependence on burning fossil fuels, and releasing the carbon stored in them, means we've been responsible for adding a lot more carbon dioxide to the air. In the past 200 years, CO_2 in the atmosphere has increased by about 25 percent. The biggest increase has taken place in the last 50 years. Some scientists predict an even greater increase in the next 20 years.

When the Sun sends **solar energy** to the Earth, about 70 percent is absorbed, and 30 percent reflects back toward space. Greenhouse gases trap some of the reflected solar energy. Greenhouse gases have always been necessary for our existence on Earth. Without them, temperatures on Earth would be about 90°F (33°C) colder, on average.

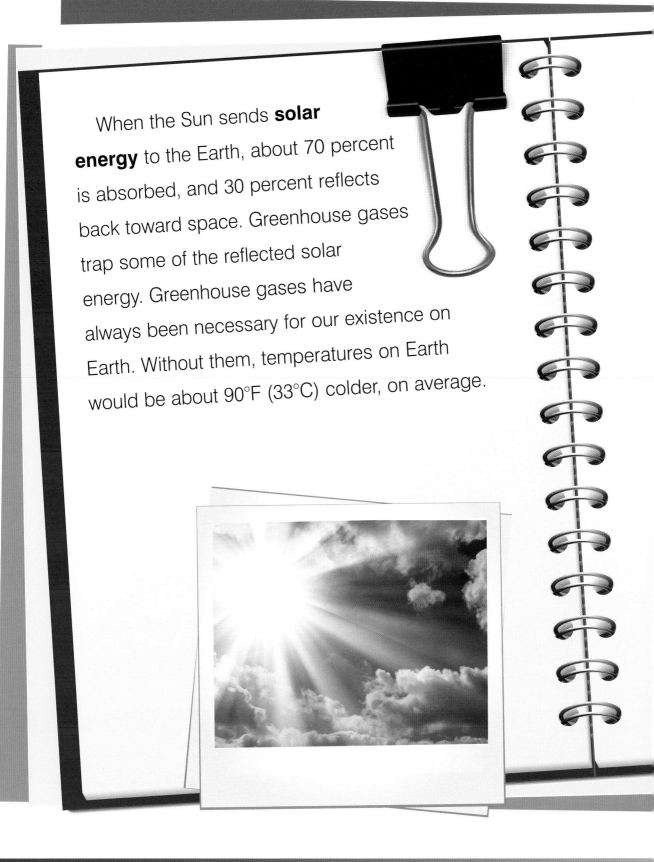

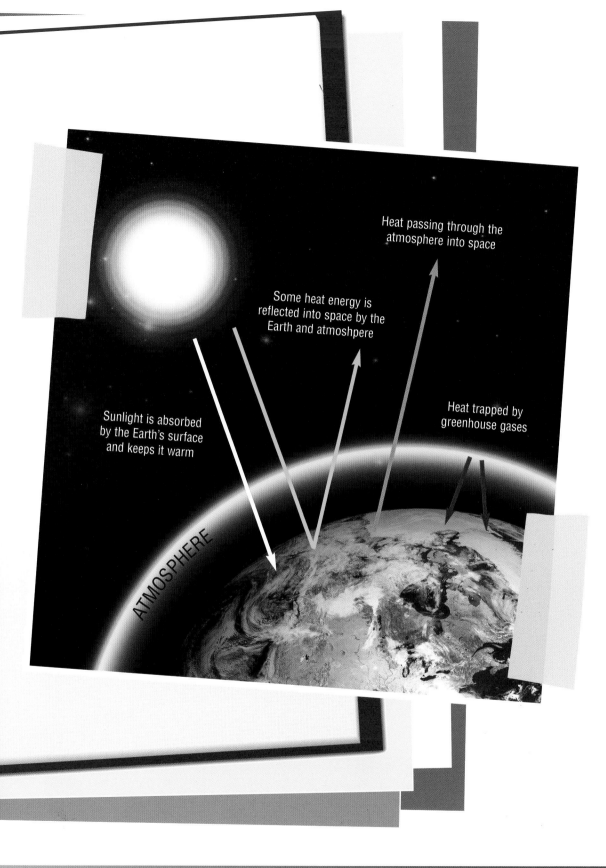

Heat passing through the atmosphere into space

Some heat energy is reflected into space by the Earth and atmoshpere

Heat trapped by greenhouse gases

Sunlight is absorbed by the Earth's surface and keeps it warm

ATMOSPHERE

In 2007, NASA reported that average worldwide temperatures have climbed 1.4°F (0.8°C) since 1880. We see the effects of warmer temperatures in disappearing Arctic ice, melting glaciers, and dying coral reefs.

AL GORE

In his book, *An Inconvenient Truth*, former Vice President Al Gore describes the effects of carbon dioxide emissions on the planet. Many people view Gore's predictions of what will happen if we continue to add greenhouse gases to the atmosphere as a call to action. He feels we must take steps to reduce **global warming** and preserve our planet.

Energy from the Sun, the wind, and the ocean's waves can help us **reduce** our use of fossil fuels. These energy sources will never run out, and they don't release carbon dioxide into the atmosphere. Switching to clean, **renewable energy** is a big step in helping our planet.

ALTERNATIVES TO FOSSIL FUELS

WIND

BIOFUEL

SOLAR

HYDRO

Rain Forests

Rain forests play an important role in the planet's health. During photosynthesis, plants take in carbon dioxide, water, and energy from the Sun. They store carbohydrates and release oxygen that we need.

Rain forests are home to many plants and animals, and they supply us with medicine and food found nowhere else on the planet.

WHERE IN THE WORLD CAN YOU FIND A RAIN FOREST?

Southern Asia

Central America

Africa

The Amazon

Australia

Rain Forests of the World

People are destroying rain forests for lumber and to make way for cattle ranching, farming, and mining. Once, tropical forests covered about 20 percent of the Earth's surface. Today, the number is closer to 7 percent.

When we cut down rain forests, we lose an important source of oxygen. On top of this, the plants and animals that depend on the rain forest die when they lose their habitat.

One bird affected by the loss of South America's rain forests are Toucans. They use their large bills to reach for fruit on small branches.

When loggers cut down all the trees in an area, the ecological results can be devastating.

CHAPTER FOUR

The Dangers of Chemical Pesticides

Farmers use chemicals to keep bugs and weeds out of their crops. We use many of the same chemicals in our gardens. They work, but they can have harmful effects on the environment. When it rains, the soil absorbs the chemicals. They enter and pollute the groundwater, a source of much of our drinking water.

A much healthier way to control pests is to use biological controls. Biological pest control uses the natural enemy of a pest to reduce its population. What if aphids are destroying your rose garden? Instead of spraying your rose bushes with pesticides, you can introduce ladybugs to your garden. The ladybugs will eat the aphids and you will have a pest-free, chemical-free garden.

RACHEL CARSON

Rachel Carson (1907-1964) was one of the first to understand the devastating effects of chemical pesticides on nature. In 1962, she published her book *Silent Spring*. The book detailed the damaging effects to wildlife caused by the use of the manmade pesticide, DDT. Carson is credited with launching the environmental movement in the United States.

CHAPTER FIVE

A Shift to Clean Energy Sources

Non-renewable energy sources, including the fossil fuels coal, petroleum, and natural gas, will eventually run out. Renewable energy sources, including energy from the Sun and wind, are not only clean sources of energy, but they exist in an endless supply. We already receive enough solar energy to fill all our energy needs; we just have to find a way to harness it so we can all use it.

This solar cell uses silicon wafers to absorb light from the Sun.

Solar cells convert the Sun's energy into electricity. They provide power to calculators, satellites, and homes. In developing countries, solar cells provide energy for more than 1 million homes. Scientists are working to find a way to use the solar energy on an even larger scale.

Solar troughs use curved mirrors to capture solar energy and direct it to a central tube. Fluid inside the tube absorbs the concentrated sunlight, is heated, and produces steam. The steam then enters a power plant and is used to produce energy.

WIND POWER

HYDROPOWER

Many scientists believe wind power can generate more than ten times the energy needed worldwide. Already, large wind farms supply electricity to thousands of homes across the United States and around the globe.

In 2007, 6 percent of electricity generated in the United States came from hydroelectric power. Hydroelectric power, or hydropower, is energy harnessed from flowing or falling water. It is currently the most widely used renewable energy source in the United States.

Biomass is organic matter made from plants and animals. We can burn it, or we can turn it into other usable forms of energy. Biomass releases carbon dioxide into the atmosphere when it burns. But when biomass crops are grown, they capture about the same amount of CO_2 through photosynthesis. This makes biomass a carbon neutral energy source.

OTHER RENEWABLE ENERGY SOURCES INCLUDE:

GEOTHERMAL ENERGY

Geothermal energy is produced by heat from the molten rock, or magma, deep within the Earth's crust; this magma often comes close to the surface where it creates volcanoes or hot springs.

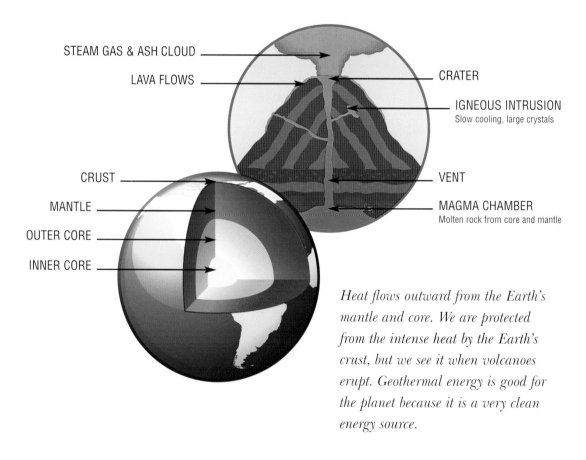

STEAM GAS & ASH CLOUD

LAVA FLOWS

CRATER

IGNEOUS INTRUSION
Slow cooling, large crystals

CRUST

MANTLE

OUTER CORE

INNER CORE

VENT

MAGMA CHAMBER
Molten rock from core and mantle

Heat flows outward from the Earth's mantle and core. We are protected from the intense heat by the Earth's crust, but we see it when volcanoes erupt. Geothermal energy is good for the planet because it is a very clean energy source.

WAVE POWER

Wave power energy is produced by the flow of waves back and forth through a turbine.

TIDAL POWER

Tidal power energy is produced when a dam catches water at high tide and then releases it through an electricity-generating turbine at low tide.

CHAPTER SIX

Personal Choices

Switching to renewable, clean energy is a big step in the right direction. But what can each of us do to reduce our negative impact on the environment? It starts with being aware of the choices we make every day.

What did you have for dinner last night? Were any of the foods grown locally?

Think about the meals you've eaten in the last week. If you stopped for dinner at a fast-food restaurant, consider the containers and wrappers used to package your food.

Some fast-food chains have taken steps to replace Styrofoam containers with cardboard boxes like this one. Elsewhere, eco-minded chains are taking it a step further by wrapping their sandwiches in uncoated paper that can go straight into the compost pile.

Once you finished eating, you put all of that packaging into the trash. Finally, sanitation workers dumped the trash in a landfill or burned it in an incinerator.

How much of your fast-food trash could have been recycled? Some of the other trash in this truck probably contains toxic metals. We need to start being more aware of the choices we make when we toss away our garbage.

Now think about all the people on Earth generating the same amount of trash from their meals. Then add in all the disposable products we've come to rely on. Since the 1960s, the amount of **solid waste** each American produces has more than doubled.

How long does it take for trash to decay, or break down?

Aluminum can	200 to 500 years
Plastic cup	250 years
Paper plate	5 years
Plastic trash bag	10 to 20 years

What if each of us made a personal pledge to cut down on disposable products? The impact could be huge!

DID YOU KNOW?

Americans throw out 60 million plastic bottles every day. That's 694 per second! Plastic doesn't disappear over time. It becomes brittle and breaks into tiny pellets. When animals eat these pellets, they can become sick and die.

SOURCE: NATIONAL GEOGRAPHIC

What can we do to reduce the amount of solid waste we generate? Some solutions are quite simple:

✓ When eating at a fast-food restaurant, take only the napkins, utensils, and ketchup packets you will use.

✓ Buy products that are sold with less packaging.

✓ **Recycle**, and buy recycled products.

✓ Use both sides of a sheet of paper.

✓ Send e-cards instead of paper cards.

✓ Use dishtowels instead of paper towels and cloth napkins instead of paper.

✓ Carry a refillable water bottle.

✓ Pack lunch foods in reusable containers instead of plastic bags, and replace throwaway paper lunch sacks with a lunch box.

Reducing our solid waste is the best way to protect the environment. But when we can't reduce our trash or find a way to reuse it, then we need to recycle it.

That picnic table where you eat your lunch might have been made from recycled plastic. And those glass bottles? They could show up in beautiful new tiles decorating a kitchen or bathroom.

Not sure what to recycle? You can find out from the local government website in the city or county where you live.

When we recycle, we turn things we can't use anymore into new materials or products. The Environmental Protection Agency estimates that 75 percent of our trash could actually be recycled. When companies make new products from recycled materials, not only do they keep trash out of landfills, but they also save energy. Aluminum can companies, for instance, use 95 percent less energy when they produce new cans from recycled materials.

Take time to recycle. You're doing great thinks for the future!

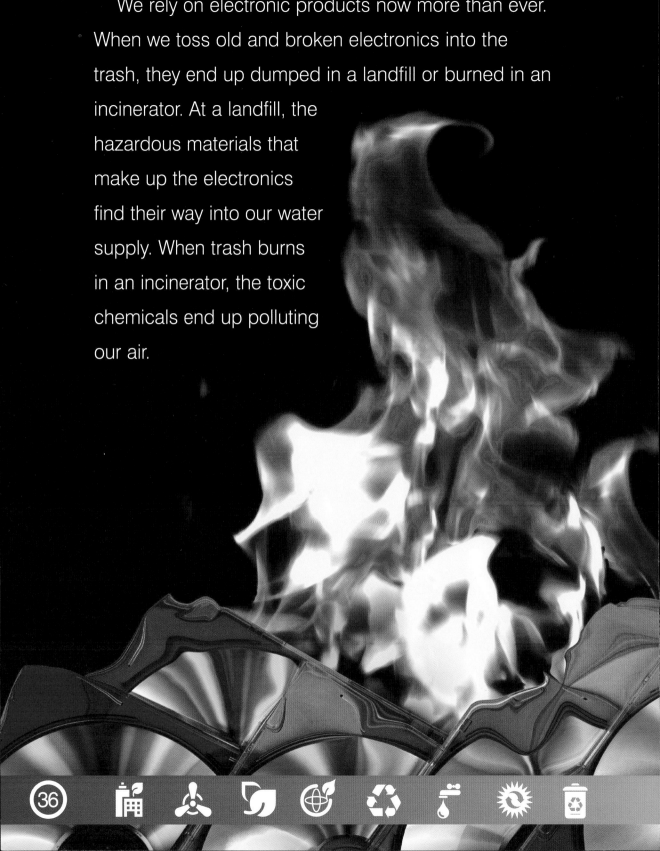

We rely on electronic products now more than ever. When we toss old and broken electronics into the trash, they end up dumped in a landfill or burned in an incinerator. At a landfill, the hazardous materials that make up the electronics find their way into our water supply. When trash burns in an incinerator, the toxic chemicals end up polluting our air.

Did you know you can raise money for charities, schools, and other organizations by recycling old ink cartridges?

There are better ways to deal with our old electronics. Instead of tossing them into the trash, give them to an electronics recycler. When you replace an ink cartridge on your printer, be sure to recycle the old cartridge. Some companies include an envelope so you can mail the cartridge directly back to them. And never throw old batteries in the trash. Schools, libraries, and other government agencies will collect them for recycling.

Americans buy more than 3 billion batteries each year. Make sure your family and friends know where to recycle them.

CHAPTER SEVEN

Your Water Footprint

How much water do you use in a day? A bath uses about 50 gallons of water. A shower, 2 gallons per minute. You'll use a gallon each time you wash your face or hands or brush your teeth. Flushing the toilet averages about 3 gallons. Don't forget about the water used in cooking, lawn watering, and clothes washing.

DID YOU KNOW?

We take about 28,433 showers in a lifetime, using about 70,000 gallons of water. That's enough water to fill four large swimming pools!

SOURCE: NATIONAL GEOGRAPHIC

We use a lot of water each day.
How can we reduce our water footprint?

✓ Take shorter showers.

✓ Turn off the water while you brush your teeth.

✓ Install low-flow showerheads, toilets, and washing machines.

✓ Fix dripping faucets. They can waste up to 4,000 gallons of water each month.

✓ Collect rainwater to water your garden.

✓ Run your sprinklers in the morning or evening. When you water your lawn in the heat of the afternoon, you lose water to evaporation.

✓ Landscape with native plants that don't require extra water or fertilizer.

We also need to keep the water supply safe. Never pour chemicals down a storm drain or onto the ground. They will end up in the groundwater that feeds into our supply of drinking water. Liquids such as paints, pesticides, and used automobile oil should be taken to a drop-off center where they will be disposed of safely.

CHAPTER EIGHT

Your Carbon Footprint

Your carbon footprint calculates the amount of carbon dioxide released into the atmosphere by your activities. Electricity and transportation can be two of the biggest producers of carbon emissions, so whenever you reduce your use of electricity, or take a bike instead of the car, you are reducing your carbon footprint.

Compact Fluorescent Light Bulb

How can you reduce your carbon footprint?

* Turn off the lights when you leave a room.

* Replace incandescent light bulbs with compact fluorescent light (CFL) bulbs.

* Turn off the T.V. set, DVD player, and computer when you're not using them. Better yet, connect them all to a power strip with an on/off switch. When you turn off electronic appliances, they go into standby mode, where they continue to use energy. You can save that energy by turning off the power supply after you turn off the appliance.

* Turn down the heat by a degree or two.

* Unplug the chargers to your cell phones and MP3 players when they are finished charging.

* Ride a bike or walk instead of taking the car.

* Plant a tree.

CHAPTER NINE

Prescription for a Healthy Planet

The best prescription for a healthy planet is for humans to leave little or no footprint on the Earth. However, this is a lofty goal that isn't easily accomplished. Fortunately, creative thinkers around the world are coming up with exciting new ideas that could help us achieve this goal.

Engineers in Australia burn biomass to generate electricity. By burning it in an oxygen-free environment, they don't allow the carbon in the biomass to escape into the atmosphere. Instead, it gets locked into the charcoal that is left after the burn.

This charcoal, called **biochar**, turns out to be a great fertilizer. When mixed into soil, it improves crop yields. Remarkably, scientists believe it might actually help reverse global warming because it locks in carbon that would otherwise end up in the air!

The warmth from sewage is another new fuel source. Sewer-heat recovery systems provide energy to heat and cool homes in Oslo, Tokyo, and other cities. Engineers in Vancouver, British Columbia, used the technology when they built the Olympic village for the 2010 Winter Olympics.

Other scientists are working to develop quieter, cleaner aircraft, **biofuels** from algae, and automobiles that run on hydrogen fuel cells. It is exciting to think that one day we might stop adding carbon dioxide to the atmosphere, and maybe even begin to reverse the damage we've already done.

Each of us leaves a footprint on the Earth. The decisions we make every day determine the size of our impact. Do what you can to reduce your footprint, and help others understand that if we all take small steps in the right direction, we *can* make a difference.

GLOSSARY

biochar (BYE-oh-char): a charcoal made when biomass is burned in an oxygen-free environment

biofuels (BYE-oh-fyoo-uhlz): plant material, manure, and other organic materials used as fuel

biomass (BYE-oh-mass): organic matter; matter that comes from living things, such as plant material and animal waste

ecological footprint (ee-kuh-LOJ-uh-kuhl FUT-print): a measure of how much of the Earth's resources are needed to support a person or a particular nation

fossil fuels (FOSS-uhl FYOO-uhlz): coal, oil, and natural gas, formed from the remains of prehistoric organisms

global warming (GLOH-buhl WORM-ing): a gradual increase in the average global temperature

greenhouse gas (GREEN-houss GASS): a gas such as carbon dioxide or methane that holds heat in the Earth's atmosphere

human footprint (HYOO-muhn FUT-print): the ecological impact of a person's life on Earth

industrial revolution (in-DUHSS-tree-uhl rev-uh-LOO-shuhn): a major change in society that came about when machines, powered by fossil fuels, were used to produce food and other products

non-renewable energy (non-ri-NOO-uh-buhl EN-ur-jee): energy sources that are limited, such as the fossil fuels coal, oil, and natural gas

recycle (ree-SYE-kuhl): to collect waste materials and use them to produce new items

reduce (ri-DOOSS): make smaller

renewable energy (ri-NOO-uh-buhl EN-ur-jee): a source of energy that can never be used up, such as energy from the wind, waves, and the Sun

solar energy (SOH-lur EN-ur-jee): energy from the Sun

solid waste (SOL-id WAYST): discarded solid material; garbage

Index

Websites to Visit

www.kidsfootprint.org/index.html

www.epa.gov/kids

www.fws.gov/endangered/kids/

www.alliantenergykids.com/stellent2/groups/public/documents

kids.mongabay.com

About the Author

Jeanne Sturm grew up exploring the woods, waterfalls, and riverbanks around her home in Chagrin Falls, Ohio. She moved to Florida and learned to windsurf, where she met her future husband. Now married, Jeanne, her husband, and their three children live in Land O' Lakes, Florida, with their dog, Astro, and bunnies, Chester and Lucy.